Energy Juices

Energy Juices

Nic Rowley and Kirsten Hartvig

DUNCAN BAIRD PUBLISHERS

LONDON

Dedication: To Kathy

Energy Juices
Nic Rowley and Kirsten Hartvig

First published in the United Kingdom and Ireland in 2000 by
Duncan Baird Publishers Ltd
Sixth Floor, Castle House
75–76 Wells Street
London W1P 3RE

Conceived, created and designed by Duncan Baird Publishers

Managing Editor: Judy Dean
Editors: Denise Alexander with Georgina Harris
Senior Designer: Steve Painter
Designer: Rachel Goldsmith
Commissioned Photography: Sian Irvine
Home Economist and Food Stylist: Pippin Britz

British Library Cataloguing-in-Publication Data:
A catalogue record for this book is available from the British Library.

10 9 8 7 6 5 4 3 2 1

ISBN: 1-900131-69-2

Typeset in Rotis Sans Serif and Univers
Colour reproduction by Colourscan, Singapore
Printed by Imago, Singapore

Publisher's Note: None of the information in this book is meant as a
substitute for professional medical advice. If you are in any doubt as to
the suitability of any of the therapeutic methods or recipes given in this
book, consult your doctor.

Follow either the imperial or the metric measurements when making the
Energy Juice recipes. The measurements are not interchangeable.

Contents

Introduction

This book is based on the oldest and most powerful of naturopathic ideas – that a well-nourished body is the key to a healthy life. By learning to extract essential goodness from fresh, organic fruits and vegetables and combine them into satisfying and invigorating drinks, we can instantly improve the nutritional quality of our diet and significantly reduce our susceptibility to disease.

Energy juices are quick and easy to make. For most fruit juices, a simple squeezer or hand press is best: gentle extraction helps preserve the quality of the juice. For vegetable juices, an electric juicer saves the time and effort of hand-grinding and pressing. For smoothies and shakes, a food processor, electric blender or hand blender can all be used. Try not to make more juice than you can use straightaway – these drinks are "live" foods which tend to lose their nutritional quality if kept for too long. Energy juices are best enjoyed in between meals (or as light snack meals in themselves) to maximize the absorption of essential nutrients into your system. Melon juices in particular should be drunk on an empty stomach.

ABOUT THE RECIPE RATING SYSTEM
All the recipes in Energy Juices are packed with natural energy. For quick reference, many of the recipes are given a star rating (maximum three stars) to make the energy benefits of these drinks immediately apparent.

chapter one

The vital flow

From earliest times, drinks and juices made from fresh fruit, vegetables and herbs have been used to relieve illness, boost vitality and improve wellbeing.

The powerful effects of fresh juices on body and mind are due in part to the high concentrations of health-enhancing chemicals they contain, but also to the fact that it is easier for the body to absorb and assimilate essential nutrients quickly and efficiently when they are taken in liquid form. By understanding the role of fluids in maintaining normal bodily function, we can use energy juices to disperse and dispel toxins from our systems, protect ourselves from minor ailments and fine-tune our diet for maximum health.

The inner sea

the essence of life

Water. It surrounds and protects us before we are born, our bodies are three-quarters made from it and our digestion and metabolism depend on it. Without it there would be no life on our planet.

In the migration from the sea to dry land, living organisms solved the physiological challenge posed by their new environment by incorporating the ocean within their tissues. Salt water became the internal medium in which materials could be transported around the body. It gave structure and solidity to cells, lubrication to moving parts, protection to delicate organs, and a way of maintaining a constant internal environment in the face of an ever-changing external world.

As evolutionary inheritors of this inner sea, we too depend on water for life and wellbeing. Our brains are 70 per cent water, our blood 60 per cent, and even our bones are 30 per cent. An "average" 155-lb (70-kg) man is made up of about 80 pints (45 litres) of water – 55 pints (30 litres) inside his cells, 20 pints (12 litres) filling the spaces between his tissues and 5 pints (3 litres) in his blood plasma.

Saliva, tears, sweat, bile, gastric juices, pancreatic fluid, cerebrospinal fluid, seminal fluid, amniotic fluid and urine all contain a high proportion of water, and the evaporation of water from the skin in the form of sweat helps to keep us cool in hot weather. The water balance in our body is closely involved in our temperature control system. In cold weather, our sweat reflex shuts down, allowing the heat from our circulation to maintain a constant internal body temperature. As the poet and philosopher J. W. von Goethe wrote: "All is born of water, and upheld by water too."

Energy juices revitalize and replenish the inner sea by ensuring that the body has access not only to the water but also to the essential nutrients it needs in a form that is easy to absorb and, just as importantly, to enjoy. Juices also encourage the elimination of metabolic wastes from our bodies. Making juices a regular part of our diet is a major step toward long-term health and vitality.

Pure and simple

What, when and how much do we need to drink for perfect health? Some natural medicine practitioners suggest that a proper diet does away with the need to drink extra fluids, while others prescribe strict restrictions on the amount we can drink. But the wisdom of most ancient healing traditions, backed up by the evidence of modern science, is that we should drink little and often throughout the day. This way, we enhance the performance of our mind and body, and avoid the build-up of toxic metabolites in our tissues.

When we are very busy, we often neglect the quiet voice of thirst. As a result, we drink too little and drinking becomes a passive activity rather than a positive contribution to health. We may abandon water and natural juices in favour of "convenient" soft drinks, containing refined sugar or caffeine. Symptoms of dehydration – a dry mouth, tiredness, irritability, concentration loss, infrequent urination, dark urine, and constipation – are accepted as a part of life.

We are constantly losing water from our bodies by evaporation when we sweat, and from our breath when we exhale. Water is also excreted in our urine and feces. If this water is not replaced, the volume of circulating plasma (which carries oxygen and nutrients to our tissues) decreases, waste in our blood becomes more concentrated, and physical and mental abilities deteriorate.

So what does this mean in practice? First, remember that drinking is healthy. Plants and animals all need water. Second, drink about $2^1/_2$ pints (1.5 litres) of pure water a day, including a small glass of water first thing in the morning and last thing at night to help keep your system running smoothly. (Drink a little water with your meals if you like, but avoid "washing down" food.) Third, exchange black tea and coffee and manufactured soft drinks for herb teas, tisanes and fresh fruit and vegetable juices, which will nourish and detoxify your body and so give you extra energy. And remember to taste what you drink – savour the flavours before you swallow.

Natural cure

juices for self-healing

In 1958, in his seminal book *A Cancer Therapy*, Dr Max Gerson wrote: "It [is becoming] more and more important that organically grown fruit and vegetables will be, and must be, used for the protection against degenerative disease and the prevention of cancer." But it is only now that we are beginning to understand the mechanisms by which plants promote our health and wellbeing.

International research has shown conclusively that increasing our consumption of fresh fruit and vegetables has a massive impact on our capacity to resist disease. From the prevention of cancer, heart disease and diabetes to protecting us from diverticulitis, hypertension, hemorrhoids and gallstones, a diet rich in plant food is an inexpensive,

practical way to avoid illness and increase vitality. This is because fresh fruits and vegetables contain phytochemicals – naturally occurring substances produced by plants to protect themselves from disease and insect damage – which have powerful, beneficial effects on human health (see p.17).

Energy juices, such as those in this book, offer the maximum opportunity to benefit from phytochemicals with minimum time and effort. As the juices are mostly based on raw ingredients, they also provide a concentrated source of the vitamins, minerals and trace elements that we need for peak performance. By using organic ingredients we avoid chemical pollution and ensure maximum nourishment as we drink.

THE VITAL FLOW

Phytochemicals
nature's health protectors

allium compounds stimulate antioxidants; destroy bacteria.

anthrocyanins are dark-coloured, antioxidant chemicals in red grapes, blueberries and cranberries. May reduce the "stickiness" of blood platelets and help prevent blood clots.

carotenoids help prevent the formation of cancer cells and may be important in determining our lifespan. They are found in yellow and orange fruits and vegetables.

coumarins stop the formation of tumours.

dithiolthyones help to maintain the health of cell membranes and the structure of chromosomes.

flavonoids are antioxidant chemicals which inhibit cancer-cell growth and may help prevent hypertension.

glucosinolates and indoles support the detoxifying action of the liver.

isoflavones help control cell growth rates.

limonene is a detoxifying chemical found in citrus fruits.

phenols inhibit the production of carcinogens.

protease inhibitors help to stop the spread of tumour cells into surrounding tissues.

saponins may help control blood cholesterol and reduce the growth rate of some tumour cells. They are found in soya products and anti-inflammatory herbs, such as chickweed.

sterols improve the health of cell membranes and may protect against colonic cancer.

thiocyanates protect DNA and block carcinogen activity.

Natural healers
the health-enhancing properties of six juice giants

beetroot Often called the "vitality plant", beetroot is rich in folate, iron and magnesium. Used to relieve all chronic illnesses, particularly those of the blood and immune system, it may also help the body to fight cancer. (Note: if you consume a lot of beetroot, your feces and urine may develop a reddish tint. This is harmless and will disappear if you reduce your intake of the food.)

carrot Extremely rich in carotenes (and a good source of fibre and chromium), carrots are traditionally used to treat digestive upsets and worms. Beta-carotene may help prevent cancer of the lungs, cervix and gastro-intestinal tract. Carrot is also thought to boost immunity, making it useful in treating chronic viral infections such as herpes simplex.

cranberry Long used to relieve urinary-tract infections, cranberry juice contains a phytochemical that prevents harmful bacteria from sticking to the bladder wall. In addition, it has powerful antioxidant effects which may improve cardiovascular health and help to prevent cancer.

red grape As well as containing anthrocyanins, which may decrease the stickiness of blood platelets and reduce the likelihood of blood clots, red grape juice also contains a compound called reservatol, which lowers blood cholesterol and may inhibit the formation of cancer cells.

orange and grapefruit The high vitamin C content of these fruits helps to maintain healthy blood cells and may increase resistance to viral infections. Vitamin C may also help to lower blood cholesterol and protect against breast cancer. (Note: the vitamin C in fresh-pressed citrus juice deteriorates rapidly – only press as much as you are going to drink straightaway.)

Clear as crystal

Clear as crystal

energy juices for brain power

Nutrition has important effects on the mind, and changes in neuro-transmitter levels caused by food can have a profound influence on mood and behaviour. For example, if we eat plenty of fresh fruit and vegetables, we increase the ratio of carbohydrate to protein in our diet. This in turn increases the availability of tryptophan, the amino acid that our brain uses to make a neuro-transmitter called serotonin. Low levels of serotonin are known to be a cause of depression, so eating more healthily can be a highly effective safeguard against a depressed mood.

Energy juices are particularly useful for keeping the brain active and alert because even though the brain comprises only 2 per cent of our total body weight, it is incredibly active metabolically and uses 20 per cent of the oxygen we breathe to sustain itself. This, plus the fact that it can use only simple glucose as "fuel", means that the brain has a particular need for energy and micronutrients in order to work efficiently. Drinking freshly made organic fruit and vegetable juices is a perfect way to ensure that we get top-quality nutrition where it is needed most – fast!

Energy juices also help to guard against the decrease in mental clarity and efficiency that minor nutritional deficiencies may cause. For example, a low intake of vitamin B_1 may result in poor sleep, restlessness, fatigue and changes in mood. A lack of vitamin B_6 is linked with anxiety, depression and pre-menstrual tension. Low levels of folate and vitamin C may cause a lowering of mood and other psychological disturbances.

A change in body potassium levels (caused by excessive intakes of tea, coffee and alcohol) leads to apathy and lethargy; and deficiencies in zinc and magnesium can lead to irritability, mood swings, poor appetite, anxiety, insomnia and fatigue. Low iron intake causes tiredness and weakness and interferes with our ability to take in new information. Insufficient chromium increases the likelihood of fatigue, anxiety and depression related to low blood-sugar levels.

chapter two

Liquid energy

In the midst of a busy life, freshly made organic juices, shakes, teas, tisanes, cocktails and smoothies can provide a sheet anchor for optimum health.

Fruits, vegetables and other natural foods contain many different nutrients, all providing us with particular benefits. Understanding what is in each ingredient of an energy juice helps us to make the best choice, so that each drink we make will give us optimum health and maximum energy. There is a juice to suit any time of day or any mood. The basic methods for each type of energy juice can be expanded on to create a myriad delicious juice recipes.

Fresh juices

In chemical terms, a fresh-pressed juice is simply a mixture of water and plant sugars plus small amounts of oils, vitamins, minerals, amino acids and phytochemicals. But these constituents can have a potent effect, helping us to fight disease and counteracting the harmful effects of medicinal drugs, caffeine, tobacco and food additives.

Fruits and vegetables contain different nutrients in varying amounts so, to help you tailor-make your own energy juices, on pages 25 and 27 we have summarized the major benefits of all the important vitamins, minerals and trace elements, together with a selection of the fruits and vegetables that are most abundant in them. But first, here are some tips on choosing and handling energy juice ingredients:

• Try to find a reliable supplier of fresh organic fruits and vegetables – herbicides, pesticides or other agrochemicals, found in conventionally farmed foods, will be concentrated in a juice, greatly diminishing its benefits and they may even be harmful to your health.

• Fresh vegetables should be firm, colourful and "alive". Bananas should be fully ripe; apricots orange-yellow blushed with pink or red; peaches weighty and fragrant; and oranges and grapefruits smooth. Look for grapes with green stems; unshrivelled guavas; firm lychees; kiwis that are slightly but uniformly soft; sweet-smelling melons and pineapples; and yielding, aromatic mangoes. Avoid strawberries with white tips, cherries that are too pale or too soft, and green paw-paws.

• Fruits and vegetables should be properly cleaned before juicing, but avoid soaking them. When removing skins, peel as finely as possible to preserve vital nutrients.

Use this table and the one on p.27 to help you to create your own special juice combinations.

VITAMIN	HEALTH BENEFITS	ENERGY JUICE SOURCES
A	Antioxidant. Keeps skin and vision healthy. Anti-cancer.	Carrots, mangoes, melons, tomatoes.
E	Antioxidant. Good for blood cells, muscles and nervous system. Protects against heart disease and some cancers.	Fresh almond milk, blackberries, hazelnuts.
K	Helps prevent osteoporosis. Ensures normal blood clotting.	Carrots, parsley, strawberries.
C	Antioxidant and anti-allergic. Improves iron absorption and wound healing. Helps immunity and blood-fat levels.	Citrus fruits, guavas, kiwis, mangoes, papayas, peaches, strawberries.
B_1 thiamin	Aids metabolism. Maintains healthy nerves and muscles.	Carrots, oranges.
B_2 riboflavin	Helps energy release from food. Keeps mucous membranes in good condition.	Fresh almond milk, blackcurrants, cherries, cucumbers, grapes.
B_3 niacin	Helps maintain optimum energy levels. Keeps skin and mucous membranes in good condition.	Apples, apricots, bananas, lemons, pears, plums, tomatoes.
B_5 pantothenate	Anti-stress. Helps maintain energy levels. Aids antibody production. Protects against hypertension and allergy.	Honey, tomatoes.
B_6 pyridoxine	Supports nervous system. Aids hemoglobin production. May protect against PMS, asthma, migraine and depression.	Bananas, elderberries, oranges, tomatoes.
Biotin	Maintains condition of skin, hair, sweat glands, nerves and bone marrow. Aids fat metabolism. Encourages appetite.	Fresh almond milk, bananas, redcurrants.
Folate	Aids growth and development of a healthy nervous system.	Apples, beetroot, carrots, oranges.
B_{12}	Supports growth. Maintains health of the blood, bone marrow and the nervous system.	Fortified soya milk.

MINERAL	HEALTH BENEFITS	ENERGY JUICE SOURCES
Calcium	Gives structure and strength to bones and teeth. Maintains health of heart, nerve and muscle tissues.	Carrots, lemons, soya milk.
Cobalt	Necessary for the normal action of vitamin B_{12}.	Apricots, cherries.
Copper	Maintains healthy red blood cells and bone and nervous tissue. May help protect against osteoporosis.	Beetroot, cherries, grapes, honey, melons, oranges, pineapples.
Fluoride	Helps preserve strong bones and teeth.	Apricots, grapes, tomatoes.
Iodine	Supports growth, metabolism and tissue repair.	Garlic, honey, lettuce.
Iron	Enables oxygen transport in the blood and muscles. Maintains energy. Supports nerves. Aids liver function.	Apples, apricots, beetroot, carrots, honey, pears.
Magnesium	Maintains bones and teeth. Protects against epilepsy, heart disease, hypertension, PMS, osteoporosis, mental illness.	Almond milk, apples, bananas, beetroot, honey, oranges, soya milk.
Manganese	Helps protein and fat metabolism. Keeps cell membranes healthy. May protect against diabetes, heart disease, epilepsy, cancer and rheumatoid arthritis.	Bananas, blackberries, carrots, celery, dandelion roots, ginger, mulberries, oranges, pears, plums.
Phosphorus	A building block for proteins, carbohydrates and fats. Supports the immune system and helps maintain energy.	Carrots, parsley, prunes, raspberries, soya milk.
Potassium	Keeps heart, muscles and nerves healthy. Boosts energy and strength.	Bananas, honey, soya milk.
Selenium	Antioxidant. Enables red blood cells to function properly.	Celery.
Zinc	Aids wound healing. Maintains skin health. Protects against prostate disorders and mental disturbances. Helps regulate blood fat levels.	Beetroot, carrots, lettuce, oranges, peaches, tomatoes.

Teas
and tisanes
infuse the goodness

Nourishing, nutrient-packed teas and tisanes made from the leaves, stems, flowers, fruits and seeds of medicinal plants have been used since the beginning of recorded history to improve health and ward off illness. Certain plants, such as mint, are caffeine-free stimulants. Others, such as camomile, aid digestion and help us to relax. Some, such as thyme, boost our natural immunity to infection and disease. All of these plants are gifts from nature – gentle, unadulterated, low-cost natural healers. Most of the plants used in traditional tisanes tend to be hardy and undemanding, and a small back garden or just a sunny windowsill are all you need to grow the ingredients for your favourite plant and herb tea mixtures (see p.64).

Make your teas in a teapot or in a cup with a lid, which will help to preserve the plant's nutritional and medicinal qualities. Use 1 cup of boiling water for each teaspoon of herb. Leave the tea to infuse for about 5 minutes. Here are 5 herbs to try:

✪ **Lemon balm** smells of honey and lemons. It heals, soothes and calms.

✪ Soothing, warming **camomile** is a good aid for the digestive system. It makes an excellent night cap, and is mild enough for children to enjoy.

✪ **Rosemary** stimulates the circulation, and helps to keep the mind clear and alert.

✪ **Sage** can relieve sore throats and reduce sweat, and helps to balance our hormones.

✪ **Yarrow** can ease the symptoms of colds and 'flu, and aids digestion and circulation.

Smoothies and shakes

a treat in a glass

Thick, cool, creamy and satisfying, pure fruit smoothies and dairy-free shakes make perfect energy boosters at any time of day, and can even be used as quick and easy substitutes for meals if time is short. They are low in fat and high in essential nutrients.

A smoothie is a mixture of fruits blended with apple, orange or pear juice into a rich, velvety, colourful drink. A shake is a combination of one or two fruits, blended with fresh almond milk or plain organic soya yogurt, and sweetened with a little maple syrup or honey to taste.

Use your favourite fruits, such as organic bananas, raspberries, mangoes or peaches, in any combination you like to make a limitless variety of health-enhancing and delicious drinks.

Here are the essentials of what you need to know to make shakes and smoothies:

✪ **Almond milk** Blanch half a cup of shelled almonds in boiling water for 2 minutes. Peel off the brown skins and dry. Grind to a fine powder. Add this to 8 fl oz/200 ml water and blend for 2 minutes. Use maple syrup to sweeten. Strain slowly through a fine mesh. In an airtight container, the milk will keep for up to 3 days in the fridge.

✪ **Smoothies** Wash and peel a cupful of your chosen fresh fruit. Add this to 8 fl oz/200 ml apple, pear or orange juice. Blend for 30 seconds. Sweeten with maple syrup or honey if necessary. For an ice-cold smoothie, blend a frozen peeled banana with the other fruit.

✪ **Shakes** Blend 1 or 2 chosen fruits (peeled and washed as necessary) and add them to 8 fl oz/200 ml fresh almond milk or organic soya yogurt. Add a tablespoon of maple syrup if you like.

Cocktails

Any combination of brightly coloured fluids can be called a cocktail, so-called because of the drink's resemblance to the multi-coloured tail feathers of a farmyard cockerel. We may think of a cocktail as an exotic drink served in bars, parties or on vacation, but its main purpose is as an apéritif – to stimulate the appetite before a delicious meal. This role is fulfilled perfectly by the clean, light flavours of blended fresh fruit and vegetable juices. What is more, by drinking energy juice cocktails you are at no risk of the negative, long-term health effects of most alcoholic cocktails.

The choice of ingredients for cocktails is limited only by our imagination. There are thousands of exotically named cocktails, alcoholic and non-alcoholic, recorded in books, magazines and the secret notebooks of expert bartenders. Use these drinks as inspiration and experiment with different fruit and vegetable combinations until you find your perfect cocktail.

A colourful, refreshing, non-alcoholic and, above all, healthy fruit-juice cocktail is perhaps a perfect way to end a busy working day and mark the beginning of a relaxed and convivial evening.

Here are some tips to help make energy juice cocktails a treat for the eye and the palate:

✪ Cocktails should be "dry"; in other words, not too sweet. Try different combinations of grapefruit, orange, pineapple, kiwi or mandarin juice sharpened with some freshly squeezed, ripe lemon or lime juice.

✪ For a savoury cocktail, try juicing 2 tomatoes, half a peeled cucumber and a stick of celery and add some lemon juice, gomasio and fresh ground black pepper to taste. For a spicier mix, add a little fresh grated ginger or a sprinkle of cayenne.

✪ Cocktails are best served cold – shake the juice ingredients together with some ice cubes in a cocktail shaker and serve immediately. For added interest, why not make ice cubes with fresh mint or lemon balm leaves "suspended" inside them – just add a leaf to each cube in the ice tray before freezing.

✪ Make your cocktails beautiful to look at. Serve them in elegant or unusual glassware and decorate with fresh fruit slices. You could garnish your drinks with fresh spearmint, lemon balm or coriander leaves, or a sprinkling of cinnamon or nutmeg.

Cordials

distilling the summer

A cordial is a sweet, concentrated juice made from fruits and/or herbs that is diluted with water before drinking. Cordials were invented by monks as a way to preserve medicinal herbs – and to make herbal remedies more palatable to their patients! In his 17th-century medical treatise, the physician and herbalist Nicholas Culpepper said of cordial that it will "... remove all weariness, heat, and tension, of the parts; therefore it is of great service in the depressed state of fevers, fatigue from excesses, and lowness of spirits".

Many liqueurs are derived from early medicinal cordials. Vermouth, for example, is named after the digestive herb wormwood and was originally drunk to aid digestion and stimulate the circulation.

Inexpensive and easy to make, home-prepared cordials preserve the goodness of summer fruits for us to enjoy long into winter.

This basic cordial recipe can be adapted to make many different-flavoured cordials, such as blackcurrant, elderberry or redcurrant.

✪ Take 2 lb/1 kg ripe berries, 1 pint/^{1}/$_2$ litre spring water, 2 tablespoons lemon juice, 1 teaspoon citric acid and 12 oz/350 g of unrefined organic cane sugar.

✪ Rinse the fruit, then place in a pan with the water, lemon juice and citric acid. Cover and heat gently until the berries burst.

✪ Strain the mixture though a cheesecloth, add the sugar and bring the liquid back to the boil. Simmer for 5 minutes.

✪ Skim off any froth, then pour the cordial into sterilized, warm glass bottles (for advice on cleaning glass bottles, refer to books on preserve making, or consult your pharmacist or a supplier of wine-making equipment). Seal and store in a cool, dark place.

✪ Drink diluted with pure water to taste.

Root drinks

The ubiquitous use of coffee as a pick-me-up and after-meal beverage is regarded by many health experts as a symptom of a stressed-out society, dependent on adrenaline and stimulants and suffering increasingly from burn-out and fatigue. Caffeine-containing drinks give us a quick burst of energy at the expense of our long-term stamina and overall vitality, and may provoke migraine headaches, as well as increasing anxiety and exaggerating the effects of stomach ulcers, hiatus hernia and arthritis.

Root drinks such as dandelion coffee (see p.58) or roasted chicory root (see below) on the other hand, make excellent replacements for traditional coffee. They improve the digestion, support the liver and help detoxify the body. In addition, root drinks have none of the negative effects of caffeine. Dandelion also acts as a general tonic and gentle laxative.

Chicory root (*Cichorium intybus*, also known as succory) was used by the Ancient Greeks and Romans to make digestive beverages, and is still a popular substitute for (and addition to) coffee in many parts of Europe. Chicory has a distinctive bitter taste, but you can sweeten your chicory coffee with a little honey if you like.

✪ You can buy ready-made roast chicory drinks and blends in good health stores but it is far more fun to grow your own chicory and transform it into a delicious drink. The best varieties are Magdeburg, Brunswick or Witloof.

✪ Chicory makes a fascinating and beautiful addition to any garden, attracting bees and butterflies in the summer. It has bright blue flowers (folk tales hold that they are the tears of a girl weeping for her lover lost at sea). The flowers open and close with such regularity that they can be used as a "floral clock". You can also use chicory as a compass – wherever it grows, the leaves always point north!

✪ To make chicory coffee, lift the roots from established plants in the late autumn. Remove any side shoots and top and tail so that each root is about 8 in/20 cm long.

✪ Wash the roots thoroughly and slice thinly. Place in a warm oven, 210–300°F/100–150°C until completely dry.

✪ Dry-fry the dried roots in a heavyweight frying pan or skillet until they are dark brown in colour – this takes about 10 minutes. Allow the roots to cool, then grind them to a fine powder using an electric coffee grinder. Use in the same way as ground coffee.

chapter three

Energy recipes

Juices suit any occasion and any time of the day. All the juices included here will lift your energy and raise your spirits, and each has specific beneficial health effects.

Fruits and vegetables are packed with all the nutrients your body needs. Each of the following energy juices provides a different combination, to benefit your body in different ways. Once you have tasted their delicious flavours, why not use the recipes as inspiration for your own juice ideas? The variety of possible blends is limited only by your personal taste and the seasonal availability of the ingredients. Each recipe makes enough juice for one generous serving.

Sunrise

1 orange
1 tangerine (keep one segment aside)
1 pink grapefruit

1. Squeeze the fruit.
2. Serve together in a tall glass
garnished with a segment of tangerine.

The high vitamin C content in this juice will help
you to fight off any infections.

Energy boost:	✪
Nutrients:	Vitamins C, B_1 & folate; copper, magnesium, manganese & zinc
Body benefits:	Tissue-healing; nervous system; bones & muscles; blood fats

Aurore

$3^1/_2$ oz/100 g raspberries
Juice of $^1/_2$ lemon
1 tablespoon maple syrup
$3^1/_2$ fl oz/100 ml soya milk

Blend all the ingredients together
and serve.

Energy boost:	✪ ✪
Nutrients:	Vitamins C & B_3; calcium, magnesium, phosphorus & potassium
Body benefits:	Immune, nervous & cardiovascular systems; bones & muscles

Orchard dawn

4 apples, peeled and cored
2 pears, peeled and cored
$1/2$ lemon, squeezed
1 teaspoon maple syrup

1. Juice the apples and pears.
2. Add the lemon juice and maple syrup.
3. Mix well and serve in a tall glass.

This is a refreshing juice that contains plenty of B vitamins and iron, which are all excellent energy boosters.

Energy boost:	✪ ✪ ✪
Nutrients:	Vitamins C, B_3 & folate; calcium, iron, magnesium & manganese
Body benefits:	Skin; mucous membranes; blood, bones & muscles; nervous system

Strawberry shake

10 strawberries, stalks removed
1 tablespoon natural soya yogurt
1 teaspoon honey (or 1 tablespoon
  maple syrup)
Pinch of vanilla powder
1 sprig fresh mint

1. Blend all the ingredients for about
30 seconds.
2. Serve garnished with a sprig of mint.

Energy boost:	✪
Nutrients:	Vitamins C, K & pantothenate; calcium, magnesium & potassium
Body benefits:	Tissue-healing; immune & nervous systems; blood, bones & muscles

Tropical shake

$^1/_2$ guava, peeled and stoned
$^1/_2$ pineapple, peeled
$^1/_2$ mango, peeled and stoned
2 lychees, peeled and stoned
1 slice of lime

1. Juice the fruits.
2. Serve in a tall glass decorated
with a slice of lime.
3. Drink through a thick straw.

Energy boost:	✪ ✪ ✪
Nutrients:	Vitamins A & C; copper
Body benefits:	Immune & nervous systems; skin; eyes; blood fats; bones

Bananarama

1 banana, peeled
1 chunk fresh coconut (or 1 teaspoon desiccated)
$3^1/_2$ fl oz/100 ml soya milk
1 teaspoon honey

1. Blend all the ingredients together for about
30 seconds.
2. Serve chilled.

Bananas are excellent for providing an instant burst of energy. Drink
this filling juice at any time of the day.

Energy boost:	✪ ✪ ✪
Nutrients:	Vitamins B_3, biotin & B_6; calcium, magnesium, manganese, phosphorus & potassium
Body benefits:	Skin & hair; bones & muscles; nervous, cardiovascular & immune systems

Apricot lassi

4 fresh apricots, peeled and stoned
1 banana, peeled
$1^1/_2$ fl oz/50 ml almond milk
1 pinch of cinnamon

1. Blend the apricots and banana with the almond milk.
2. Serve garnished with a pinch of cinnamon.

A lassi is a traditional drink in India, where it is known for its cooling,
refreshing properties.

Energy boost:	✪ ✪ ✪
Nutrients:	Vitamins E, B_2, B_3, B_6 & biotin; cobalt, fluoride, iron, magnesium, manganese & potassium
Body benefits:	Immune, nervous & cardiovascular systems; bones & muscles; teeth

Peach pleaser

2 fresh peaches, peeled and stoned
2 fresh apricots, peeled and stoned
$1^1/_2$ fl oz/50 ml soya milk
1 tablespoon maple syrup
1 pinch vanilla powder

Blend all the ingredients together and serve.

Energy boost:	✪ ✪
Nutrients:	Vitamins C & B_3; calcium, cobalt, fluoride, iron, magnesium, phosphorus, potassium & zinc
Body benefits:	Immune & cardiovascular systems; skin; bones & teeth; tissue-healing

Ace

9 oz/250 g carrots
1 orange, squeezed
$^1/_2$ lemon, squeezed

1. Juice the carrots.
2. Add the orange and lemon juice, mix well and serve.

This juice is packed with antioxidants to help the body fight infection.

Energy boost:	✪ ✪
Nutrients:	Vitamins A, K, C, B_1, B_3, B_6 & folate; calcium, copper, iron, magnesium, manganese, phosphorus & zinc
Body benefits:	Immune, cardiovascular & nervous systems; blood & bones; skin; tissue-healing

G&T

1 ruby-red grapefruit
3$\frac{1}{2}$ fl oz/100 ml Indian tonic water
1 slice of lemon

1. Juice the grapefruit and pour into a tall glass.
2. Add tonic water.
3. Garnish with a slice of lemon.
4. Serve with plenty of ice.

Energy boost:	✪
Nutrients:	Vitamin C
Body benefits:	Immune system; blood fats

Melon magic

$\frac{1}{4}$ water melon
$\frac{1}{4}$ cantaloupe melon
$\frac{1}{4}$ honeydew melon
1 pinch of cinnamon

1. Peel and seed the melons.
2. Blend together. Serve poured over ice cubes in a tall glass.
3. Garnish with a sprinkle of cinnamon.

Energy boost:	✪ ✪
Nutrients:	Vitamin A; copper
Body benefits:	Skin; immune & nervous systems; blood & bones

Tim's toms

2 large fresh tomatoes
1 teaspoon tamari
1 pinch fresh thyme
Salt, pepper and tabasco to taste
1 slice of lemon

1. Juice the tomatoes.
2. Stir in the tamari, thyme, salt, pepper and tabasco.
3. Pour into a glass and float the slice of lemon on top.

Energy boost:	✪
Nutrients:	Vitamins A, B$_3$, pantothenate & B$_6$; fluoride & zinc
Body benefits:	Immune & nervous systems; skin; bones; teeth; tissue-healing

Glamorgan glee

1 cup peppermint tea
$1/2$ teaspoon lemon zest
1 pinch cinnamon
1 whole clove
$1/2$ teaspoon fresh grated ginger
1 teaspoon maple syrup
1 orange, squeezed
Fizzy water and ice cubes to taste
Fresh mint and slice of lemon

1. Make the peppermint tea.
2. While it infuses, place the lemon zest, cinnamon, clove and ginger in a bowl or large cup.
3. Add the maple syrup, orange juice and brewed peppermint tea.
4. Leave to cool.
5. Just before serving, add fizzy water and ice cubes.
6. Garnish with fresh mint and a slice of lemon.

Energy boost:	✪
Nutrients:	Vitamins C, B$_6$ & folate; copper, magnesium & manganese
Body benefits:	Immune, digestive, nervous & cardiovascular systems

Starburst

$3^{1}/2$ fl oz/100 ml water
1 teaspoon honey
1–2 whole cloves
1 teaspoon fresh grated ginger
1 pinch cinnamon
1 piece star anise
1 orange, peeled
2 thick pineapple slices, peeled
1 slice of lime
Ice cubes

1. Pour the water into a small saucepan. Add the honey and spices.

2. Bring to the boil, turn the heat down and simmer, stirring occasionally, until the liquid reduces by half. Strain and leave to cool.
3. Juice the orange and pineapple. Mix with the cooled liquid.
4. Serve with the lime and ice cubes.

Energy boost:	✪ ✪
Nutrients:	Vitamins C, B$_6$ & folate; copper, magnesium, manganese & zinc
Body benefits:	Immune & nervous systems; blood, skin & bones; tissue-healing

Apple fizz

4 eating apples, peeled and cored
$^1/_2$ lemon, squeezed
4 fl oz/100 ml sparkling mineral water
Ice cubes

Energy boost:	✪ ✪ ✪
Nutrients:	Vitamins C, B$_3$ & folate; calcium, iron & magnesium
Body benefits:	Immune, nervous & cardiovascular systems; bones

1. Juice the apples.
2. Add the lemon juice.
3. Pour into a serving glass, add sparkling water and ice cubes and serve.

Research shows that regularly eating apples improves breathing by increasing lung capacity.

Lemon spring

Juice of a lemon
1 tablespoon honey
Still or sparkling mineral water to taste
1 sprig lemon balm
Ice cubes

Energy boost:	✪ ✪
Nutrients:	Vitamins B$_3$ & C; calcium
Body benefits:	Immune system; skin; bones

1. Pour the lemon juice into a glass.
2. Add the honey to the lemon juice and mix well.
3. Dilute with the water, add ice cubes, and serve with a floating sprig of lemon balm.

When lemon juice was added to sailors' rations in 1772 scurvy vanished from the British Navy within two years.

Elderflower "champagne"

The creamy-white blossoms of the graceful elder herald the beginning of summer, and have a long history of medicinal use by traditional herbalists. They are considered to have "hot and dry" properties, making them excellent protectors against colds and 'flus and useful in easing chronic conditions such as arthritis. They also help the body to detoxify by improving circulation and encouraging perspiration. Fragrant and relaxing, elderflower champagne is a delicious way to promote good health.

1 head of fresh elderflowers
1 thick slice of lemon
2 teaspoons maple syrup
4 fl oz/100 ml boiling water
Fizzy water to taste

1. Place the elderflowers in a small bowl and
pour the boiling water over.
2. Add the lemon slice and maple syrup.
3. Cover and leave to cool.
4. Strain and dilute 50/50 with chilled fizzy water
just before serving.

Energy boost:	✪ ✪
Nutrient:	Vitamin C
Body benefits:	Upper respiratory system

Dandelion coffee

You can buy dried dandelion roots from a healthfood store, or, between September and April, you can dig your own roots from the garden and dry them as follows:

2 or 3 dandelion roots

1. Wash the fresh roots and cut into short pieces.
2. Place them in a warm oven (225–300°F/100–150°C) for several hours until completely dry.
3. Place the dried roots in a dry, heavy-weight frying pan. Heat over a moderate heat.

4. Stir continuously until they turn a rich, dark brown.
5. Grind the roots in a coffee grinder. Store in a sealed container.
6. Brew and serve like regular coffee.

Benefits:

Dandelion coffee is a renowned tonic for the liver and digestion. It also benefits the cardiovascular system and is detoxifying.

Anisette

1 star anise
2 sprigs of fresh lemon balm
Boiling water

1. Place the anise star and lemon balm sprigs in a tea cup.
2. Pour boiling water over to fill cup.
3. Leave to infuse for 5 minutes.
4. Remove one of the lemon balm sprigs and serve immediately.

Benefits:

Star anise, a general stimulant, benefits the lungs as well as digestion, while the lemon balm relaxes the body and raises the spirits.

Sweet fennel

Sweet fennel is a relaxing and sweet-smelling aromatic herb, and a soothing digestive remedy suitable for all ages. It is said traditionally to increase the flow of milk in nursing mothers and, since its calming influence on the digestion passes to the baby with the breast milk, it also helps to ease infant colic.

Camomile flowers, with their distinctive scent of apples, are renowned for their gentle healing effects and for their ability to calm body, mind and spirit. Combined with sweet fennel and a little licorice, they make a delicious digestive drink that can be enjoyed at any time of day, and especially after meals.

$^1/_2$ teaspoon fennel
$^1/_2$ teaspoon camomile
$^1/_2$ teaspoon licorice
8 fl oz/200 ml boiling water

1. Place the herbs in a small, clean teapot.
2. Pour a cup of boiling water over them.
3. Leave to infuse for 5 minutes.
4. Strain and serve in a tea cup.

Benefits:
This herbal blend has a soothing and calming effect on the digestion, gently relieving indigestion and colic. It also benefits the respiratory system.

Sleepy time

$1/2$ teaspoon camomile flowers
$1/2$ teaspoon cowslip flowers
$1/2$ teaspoon lime flowers
8 fl oz/200 ml boiling water

1. Put the herbs in a small teapot.
2. Add the boiling water.
3. Cover and leave to infuse for
5–10 minutes.
4. Strain and serve.

Benefits:
This relaxing herbal blend benefits the digestive and nervous systems. Its anti-stress and mildly sedative properties naturally encourage restful sleep.

Hot cinnamon

$1^3/_4$ in/2 cm long piece of cinnamon
 (or 1 teaspoon ground)
8 fl oz/200 ml rice milk
1 teaspoon honey

1. Place the cinnamon and rice milk in
a small saucepan. Bring to the boil.
2. Simmer for a couple of minutes.
3. Pour into a mug and add the honey.
4. Drink immediately.

Benefits:
A warming and soothing bedtime drink which also aids digestion.

Thyme

A native of sundrenched mountain slopes, thyme thrives on warmth and well-drained soil. It makes an excellent aromatic tea with a warm, clove-like flavour.

A few young thyme shoots
8 fl oz/200 ml boiling water

1. Place the thyme in a teapot.
2. Add the boiling water.
3. Leave to infuse for 5 to 10 minutes.
4. Strain and serve.

Benefits:
Thyme benefits the digestive, respiratory and immune systems. Its antiseptic and antibiotic properties have been known and valued since ancient times.

Mint

Mint is particularly well suited to growing on a windowsill. Keep the soil moist and don't let it grow too tall – 6 in (15 cm) is about right. Mint tea soothes the digestion and stimulates the body and mind – the perfect after-meal pick-me-up.

A few leaf tips of mint
8 fl oz/200 ml boiling water

1. Place the mint leaves in a teapot.
2. Add the boiling water.
3. Leave to infuse for 5 to 10 minutes.
4. Strain and serve.

Benefits:
Mint, a general stimulant, benefits the nervous and immune systems. The cool, refreshing taste of fresh mint tea makes it a perfect after-dinner digestive.

Vital force

9 oz/250 g fresh beetroot
$^1/_2$ in/1 cm piece of fresh horseradish
$^1/_2$ grapefruit

1. Juice all three ingredients
and mix well.
2. Pour into a small tumbler and
serve garnished with a little extra
grated horseradish.

Beetroot is widely used by herbalists and naturopaths
to help relieve chronic illness and increase vitality.

Energy boost:	✪ ✪
Nutrients:	Vitamins C & folate; copper, iron, magnesium & zinc
Body benefits:	Immune system; blood; tissue-healing; blood fats; detoxifying

Deep heat

1 thick slice of lemon
1 piece of fresh ginger, $^2/_3$ in/1.5 cm
    long, peeled and bruised
8 fl oz/200 ml boiling water

1. Place the lemon and ginger in a
large tea cup or rice bowl.
2. Add the boiling water and leave to
infuse for a couple of minutes.
3. Remove the lemon and ginger with
a spoon. Drink immediately.

Known as the "garlic of the East", ginger is a
natural antibiotic and circulatory stimulant.

Energy boost:	✪
Nutrients:	Vitamins B_3 & C; calcium, magnesium & potassium
Body benefits:	Immune, digestive & cardiovascular systems

A plus

17$^1/_2$ oz/500 g carrots
1 stalk celery
1 small bunch parsley

1. Juice all the ingredients together. Reserve some
parsley for garnishing.
2. Serve in a tall glass with the reserved
parsley sprinkled on top.

Energy boost:	✪ ✪
Nutrients:	Vitamins A, K, B$_1$ & folate; calcium, iron, manganese, phosphorus, selenium & zinc
Body benefits:	Immune, cardiovascular & nervous systems; tissue-healing; skin; bones & muscles; blood

High C

5 oz/150 g redcurrants
5 oz/150 g blackcurrants
2 tablespoons natural organic soya yogurt
1 pinch of fresh grated ginger

Blend all the ingredients together. Serve chilled.

Energy boost:	✪
Nutrients:	Vitamins B$_2$, C & biotin; calcium, magnesium, phosphorus & potassium
Body benefits:	Immune & nervous systems; skin & hair; mucous membranes; blood

timely juices throughout the year

Spring

½ cucumber	1 handful
1 spring onion	dandelion leaves
2 carrots	1 pinch thyme
1 stick celery	1 pinch salt

1. Juice the cucumber, spring onion, carrots, celery and dandelion leaves.
2. Add the thyme and salt. Mix well.
3. Serve chilled.

Energy boost:	✪ ✪
Nutrients:	Vitamins A, K, B_2 & folate; calcium, iron, manganese & zinc
Body benefits:	Digestive, urinary & immune systems; detoxifying

Summer

Juice of ½ lemon	2½ fl oz/75 ml
A few lemon balm	apple juice
sprigs	2½ fl oz/75 ml
A few mint sprigs	fizzy water

1. Crush the herbs and add to the lemon juice. Pour into a tall glass.
2. Add the apple juice and fizzy water.
3. Serve chilled.

Energy boost:	✪
Nutrients:	Vitamins C, B_3 & folate; calcium, iron & magnesium
Body benefits:	Immune & nervous systems; skin; blood

Autumn

1 bunch of muscat grapes
1 carrot
1 teaspoon hazelnut paste

1. Juice the grapes and the carrot.
2. Add the hazelnut and serve chilled.

Energy boost:	✪ ✪ ✪
Nutrients:	Vitamins A, E, K, B_1, B_2, B_3, biotin, B_6 & folate; calcium, copper, fluoride, iron, magnesium, manganese, phosphorus, potassium & zinc
Body benefits:	Whole-body nutritional workout

Winter

1 beetroot	1 pinch of cumin
1 carrot	1 small pinch salt
1 small leek	Ice cubes

1. Juice the beetroot, carrot and leek.
2. Add cumin and salt. Serve with ice.

Energy boost:	✪
Nutrients:	Vitamins A, K, B_1 & folate; calcium, copper, iron, magnesium, phosphorus & zinc
Body benefits:	Blood; immune & nervous systems; detoxifying

Index

Acknowledgments
The authors would like to thank Allan Hartvig, Françoise Nassivet, François Salies, Geoffrey Cannon, Jaqueline Young, Jennifer Maughan, Joyce Thomas, Judy Dean, Kathy Mitchison, Lilly Jensen, Linda Wilkinson, Peter Firebrace, Ric Wilkinson, Sue Mitchison and Tessa Hodsdon for their help and inspiration in writing this book.

The authors' website is at www.labergerie.net.